Book One

The Energy of Money
How To Catch The Flow of Abundance

Everything is comprised of energy. Ongoing Creation is the result of an unimpeded flow of infinite energy. Once you understand how energy is rightly to be used, "Right-use-ness™," you too can participate in and benefit from the highest manifestation of you own capacity to create abundance.

In this first book of the series ***Awakened Consciousness: Everyday Application of Universal Principles*** we explore how to magnetize and utilize true wealth. One aspect of wealth is money. It too, is energy. Like energy, money performs best when it flows...changing hands, stimulating growth, and uplifting the downtrodden. However, before you can release the flow of money you must first understand how to acquire it. This has less to do with financial acumen than it does to understanding the basic Universal Principles that apply to energy.

In ***The Energy of Money*** we will apply Universal Principles as they relate to money, wealth and abundance through our own personal experiences as well as the successful application of these same Principles by others.

Show me the mental picture you have of yourself and we will know how you use and manifest energy. A negative self-image creates a blockage in your ability to receive and transmit energy. Think of it as a drain pipe intended to act as a conduit for water. Now place an obstruction in that pipe and what do you get? If you said "a mess" you were right! Everything backs up and flow is either reduced or cut off completely. Its intended use, its *right-use-ness™*, is unable to function. This is what a negative self-image does to your ability to be creatively abundant.

However once the blockage is removed, whether it be the garbage in the drain pipe or your limiting self-image, the natural design function and flow resume.

Self-image correction...making it bigger, brighter and more powerful...brings you face-to-face (literally!) with your real self, not the one you formerly created that has limited your and cheated you of the success and abundance that is your birthright.

I, Carole, am a philosopher and mystic at heart. I, Steve, am a practical man. All the tips and tricks we share with you are things we do regularly. However vital "doing" is it's the second half of the equation. The first half requires an understanding of what needs to be done and why.

Without both parts, understanding and action, you will come up short of your goals. Higher understanding combined with consistent and concentrated action is the key.

The nuts and bolts of investing and smart business tactics abounds. Here, we intend to unlock for you a timeless mechanism facilitating the Right-use-ness™ of the energy of money.

We each have a brain and yet we are so much more than that. Our brain is but a tool. The source of knowledge regarding the Right-use-ness™ of that tool exists well beyond the brain. Let's once and for all expose the "wizard behind the curtain" and put to rest the illusion that simply hard work and savings will make you rich. While there is a process for achieving riches, it's about so much more than the interest rate, the Dow, and how many hours you are willing to enslave yourself to a false narrative.

So now... the Right-use-ness™ of money!

1. Honor Your Word

A few years ago I went to a conference in Chicago offered by the Institute of Self Actualization. One of the main principles I came away with, that I still use today, was to honor my word. The quality of my life is dependent on the quality of my commitments. If I say that I am going to call someone, then I call them. If I tell someone that I want to have lunch with that person, then I set the date and keep it. Further, I have learned to bring the same level of integrity and consistency to the commitments I make to myself as to those I make to others. For example, one of my commitments is that I pray the rosary every day without fail; it only takes 10 minutes and it leaves me grounded and centered for the day. If I were to not keep that commitment on any given day, I am the one who suffers. Not only do would I miss the grounding, I have shown myself by my inaction that my word is unreliable.

Steve

As a mystic and Intuitive, I have always been in search or more and deeper meaning to the questions life presents. To that end I took a course in Kabballah, Jewish mysticism, about 15 years ago. I remember the instructor, a Rabbi, talking about the importance of following through with your word. He said that once we say something...it is as if that which we spoke has already occurred...that the manifestation of sound is instantaneous. It is only here in our four dimensional reality (length, width, depth and specifically, *time*) that we experience a distance or lag between that which we speak and it actual occurrence. So, he added, when you say something and *do not follow through with its corresponding action*, you create havoc and chaos because other occurrences already lined up that naturally followed from the words you spoke and now they are in chaos in the absence of your action.

Carole

Problem: As we shared above, each time you do not keep a commitment to yourself you lied to yourself. You know precisely what it was you did not do. That knowing leads to feelings of guilt, mistrust of self and lowered self-esteem. Mistrust of self gets projected outward as mistrust of others. Both the negative feelings you harbor for yourself and their projection onto others keep you from actualizing the very relationships and opportunities you are most likely seeking. That "game" also keeps you from growing as an individual.

Solution: We suggest that you start keeping your commitments. However, in the beginning, keep those commitments to a minimum that you can follow through with and but be firm in honoring them. As you begin to honor your basic commitments just watch and begin to notice the powerful results. As you become more reliable and dependable, people will rely and trust you for the things *they* need to accomplish in their lives. What follows is a profound shift towards genuine intimacy in your relationship and expansion of opportunities to prosper.

2. Make Every Day a "Yes" Day

In 2006, after a successful 8 years in trading bonds, I was moved to a sales desk to resurrect a dormant account-base spread throughout Latin America and the Caribbean. Given that I was making money there was no reason for me to move. However, given that Wall Street can be like the mafia, they made me an offer I couldn't refuse. You see Wall Street is a numbers game; make your sales and you are fine. If not, you'll be shown the door. To make matters worse, the new account base was out of Latin America. It would take me months to open new accounts. I wasn't sure if my superiors were setting me up for failure or not. I focused on my reality: no business and no clients meant I'd be doomed. All I had in my tool box was my energy and my determination to create a positive outcome. I would get up early every day and focused on what I wanted. It was my ability to say "Yes" that transformed the business. When I left the firm in 2010, I left them with one of the most profitable account bases they ever had.

Steve

My parents had opposite philosophical perspective on life. My father saw the glass *more than* half full. He would actually cross out the word "can't" whenever he came across it in a book. He believed in unlimited potential. My mother, to the contrary, worried a great deal and focused upon lack as she saw the glass *less than* half empty. For the greater part of my life, I internalized and acted upon my mother's view. The thing about how we see the world is that through our perspective we actually *assure* its continuation. When I finally realized what my view was creating, I re-evaluated things and began to see the "glass of life" as my father had. Sure enough, as it had created abundance and peace for him it now does the same for me. I awaken each day filled with certainty for the abundant possibilities that await me.   *Carole*

Problem:

We have a tendency to select by default. Our "default drive" is often the easiest but rarely the most productive path to travel. It's also often part of a pattern of behavior that we've either inherited or learned from others who were similarly trapped in their own lives.

Solution

Our ability to participate in the flow of creation resides in the fact that we are both receivers and transmitters of energy. This process is magnetic. We literally draw towards us that which we are. We also send out that which we are. If you want to magnetize more positive flow into your life, start the day with a resounding "Yes" to life. Upon awakening each day, have your first thought be "Yes, I can and I will!! Literally make that statement out loud! Now you have tuned into the frequency on which your day will proceed. Awakening and focusing upon what you cannot do and will not accomplish also tunes you into a frequency; however, it's the frequency of stagnation and deterioration. Since you were given Free Will, why not use it to *choose* what frequency you intend to receive and transmit energy on each and every day of your life?

3. Believe and Think That You Can

I always wanted to be a black belt in a Martial Art. As a kid I learned a variety of different styles which included wrestling, hapkido, karate and tae kwon do before settling on Aikido. I started training in Aikido when I was in my twenties. But from the time I first stepped onto the mat, I knew I would achieve black belt. I trained every day for years and many days twice a day. Given that Aikido can be brutal, along the way I ended up having two shoulder surgeries, two knee surgeries and twelve years of classes before I became a black belt. Had I focused on the injuries or the time it took I would have never accomplished my goal. I believed I could do it and I did. The mindset that I took in getting my black belt is the same one that I use in the acquisition of money.

Steve

When I was growing up I always thought I would be a lawyer. In fact, I wrote an essay in 5th grade that my parents saved. It says, "When I grow up I am going to become a lawyer. Of course, I'm going to become a wife and mother… but first I'm going to be a lawyer." What happened? I went to law school. While in my second year of law school, I became ill and was housebound for almost a year. I remember my nephew saying at the time, "Well, she'll never finish now." I also remember thinking how wrong he was. I knew I would recover. In fact, during that year I often "saw" myself accepting my diploma at graduation and imagined how that moment would feel! Once recovered, I returned to school and became a lawyer. Years later, as I had written in 5th grade, I married and we adopted our daughter.

Carole

Problem

Too often we think about and emotionally experience failure. We literally apply our energy to assure we will get exactly what we do *not* want. We focus on obstacles, impediments, and a myriad of reasons why "its" not likely to happen… why we will not succeed or attain our desired goal.

Solution:

Always carry the unwavering belief and mental picture that you can do what it is you want to do. Even if you have never done it before, and the likelihood of success is minimized by others or obstacles appear along the way, your unwavering belief and mental out-picturing will lead you to take the necessary actions to make it happen. Magnetizing or attracting money is no different. If you believe you can't succeed, the negative emotions and defeatist thinking that accompanies such thoughts will prove you right. In fact, that approach actually has you failing before you start! Negative thinking robs you of the passion to manifest your desires. Passion is the fuel that nourishes the engine of your thoughts. Remember this formula: Imagination + Passion + Action = Success. Hopefully the success you seek is to prosper at doing what you love. If so, remember **IPAS**!

4. Pay Your Bills with a Thankful Attitude

Having lived and traveled to poor countries, I am always thankful for the blessings that I have. I give thanks every day for having a roof over my head because I have been in houses where the roof was made of thatch. I have been in houses with no indoor plumbing or indoor water and I always give thanks that I live in a house that has both. When I get bills for the services that I use I always do it out of a spirit of gratitude because I have access to those wonderful amenities as well I have the ability to afford them. I never take these things for granted. I am thankful for having the ability to pay for these luxuries and having been able to afford them because I know many people in the world cannot.

Steve

I'm know I'm not alone in how I used to dread having to sit down and tackle the month's bills that needed to be paid. Similarly, when spending a significant amount of money I did it... but with a somewhat guilty feeling or heavy heart because I "shouldn't be purchasing something that cost that much." Then one day I combined my own experience with some advice a friend gave me. As for my experience, I realized how good I felt once the bills *were* paid. How liberated I felt and the relief I experienced from the ensuing feeling of no longer avoiding what needed to be done. So I began to look forward to clearing out the bills because I focused instead upon the positive reward awaiting me when I finished. As for spending money, regardless of amount, a friend once told me "think of all the people you are helping who were part of creating that item and be grateful for the opportunity to help in that way."

Carole

Problem:

We take on obligations while making believe or denying to ourselves that there will be responsibilities that accompany obligations. Responsibilities are often seen as negatives. They are perceived as "burdens" we "dread" and so do everything we can to stall having to face them. Avoidance only adds stress to what we already see as a stressful situation.

Solution

When we dig deep, it's always true that we can identify a reason for gratitude buried in our responsibilities. Sometimes we have to dig deeper than others but inevitably, we reach the gift that's been bestowed upon us. In the example of bills, instead of dreading writing those checks, say the following: "Thank you, God, for the bills I have and thank You for providing me with the abundance with which to pay them." Think of the bills as being both 1) a cost of being alive and 2) a part of the frequency flow of energy you are choosing to participate in. As you thank God/Universe for giving you the ability to pay the debts, you are identifying and defining the energy as something positive. When you think and say these words really feel the emotion. In that instant you transmute negative energy into positive energy. The Universe, in its desire to meet your needs, will then provide you more money to meet your obligations and continue in the flow. Remember, it isn't change that causes stress. Its *resistance* to change that causes it.

5. Expect Financial Surprises

The typical American mindset is that the only way to make money is from hard work and effort. If I were to believe that I would be cutting off the flow of money that can come in a variety of different ways. For example, my wife and I are regularly given clothes and kids' toys by everybody. I have been given brand new clothes by people I don't even know. I rarely buy clothes for my kids because I am always being given them. With 6 kids, this has been a huge windfall for me. Also, over the course of my career, I have acquired clients from a multitude of ways that never required cold calling or pounding the pavement. These clients brought me a multitude of money, and deals, that I could never had acquired on my own had I believed that only hard work and effort could bring me riches. The fact that I was open to receiving these unexpected surprises brought me more of them.

Steve

My ex-husband worked for the same company for 45 years. He received a weekly paycheck while building a 401(k) retirement plan and pension. It was how he defined responsibility and earnings. When I ceased to practice law, he became upset and panicked at the termination of monthly income from my practice. Despite the fact that over the course of the next few years I brought in to our financial situation significant amounts of money...he could not value the process because the arrival times and amounts were sporadic based upon consulting or other types of enterprises in which I chose to devote my energy. I had been raised by an entrepreneur who believed in compensation tied to your personal effort. For me, as long as the end product was sufficient, a pattern of regularity was not. I expected sufficiency not regularity.

Carole

Problem

We are creatures of habit and develop mindsets about how and when things should happen. This is most limiting when it comes to the flow of abundance. God/Universe is infinitely creative and abundant. When we limit our receptivity to this reality we instantly cut off the flow of that infinite abundance and the possibility of receiving its bounty is blocked.

Solution

Believe that income can come from anywhere. Even believe that it can be unexpected! Believing you can receive unexpected income is a powerful and liberating concept. It enables you to stop relying on historical or accepted channels of income to be your only money supply.

Instead you will come to believe money can come to you in any form, fashion or method (assuming legally and morally). Money can even show up for no reason whatsoever... other than the fact that you opened yourself to the possibility of it coming to you. Sometimes you find money lying around that you forgot you even had. Or somebody will present a job opportunity to you out of the blue that isn't even in your field and it pays well. Or somebody might suggest and idea that leads you both to an awesome business deal that will enable each of you, and eve others, to prosper. This unexpected income will come to you if you magnetize this mindset, dare to think differently and open to the flow of the unexpected.

5. Learn How to Magnetize Money

When I was first introduced to the concept of magnetizing money I started small, focusing on pennies. Wherever I would go I'd try and see how many pennies I could collect. It's actually easy to do. I would look at the floor wherever I went and I always found change. Instead of just attracting pennies, soon I was attracting nickels, dimes and quarters. After I could do that easily I began to focus on dollars. Now my focus would have to be more expansive in order to attract dollars. So I expanded my thinking and as I did, different opportunities came my way. I began attracting dollars to me every day! For example, during this time I had a business owner approach me about putting a vending machine in his store. Within a few weeks I had a cold drink machine that was paying me over $ 30 dollars a day. After I knew I could bring in dollars, I focused on attracting *thousands* of dollars into my life. Once again, I had to think meditate and ponder how accomplish this. In the end I succeeded once again by offering consulting services for my business...something I had never done before. It, too, worked. Remember, if this concept is new to you start small. You will grow your abundance as you grow your perspective.

Steve

For the greater part of my life I never thought about money or worried about it. I was raised by an affluent family and my father in particular, whom I admired, seemed to be a magnet for success. Money came easily to him. What I noticed was that he worked at what he loved, put all his profits back into the business he loved, and gave money away freely to those in need. It seemed to me he rode a natural rhythm or flow which, through his passion and generosity, attracted to him more and more money in a never ending stream. Similarly, in her own way, my mother lived a version of this. She loved slot machines and buying lottery tickets. Not as an addiction but as sheer fun. So once a month or so she would go to a casino in a nearby state for a few hours of enjoyment. I have never in my life seen anyone win as regularly as she did... at slots and lotteries! In fact, when in her lifetime she never hit a "big lotto" for millions of dollars, I heard her say with all seriousness, on more than one occasion, "I don't understand why I haven't won yet!" It was as if her will gdrew or magnetized money to her.

Carole

Problem:

Because we do not regularly associate money with energy, we overlook its magnetic quality. We think of money as the end product of hard work or sporadic luck without "connecting the dots" that link it to the power and flow of the Universe and all its creative possibility. Thinking of money as a stagnant noun rather than an energetic verb always seeking out its next rightful transit in the cosmic flow of creative transmission and reception inhibits your ability to be a recipient of that flow.

Solution

You want to identify and align with the magnetic quality of money that is unique to you. Whether it is your focused intention and determination to make yourself available to attract pennies, nickels, dimes, dollars, and ultimately, thousands of dollars... or passionately pursuing what you love... or simply never wavering from your expectation that you are a money magnet for sheer luck... establishing your end of the magnetic pole is vital to crating the current through which money can flow.

7. Speak the Word and Be Thankful in Advance

Here are some of the words that I speak over my life every day:

- I am a money magnet.
- I find favor wherever I go.
- God's wealth is circulating in my life.
- All my needs desires and goals are met instantaneously for I am one with God and God is everything.
- All that I own is paid for. I owe no man anything except to love him.
- Each and every day I am attracting more and more money into my life.

Whenever I get any type of windfall I thank God for the money, no matter how large or small the amount might be. If I find a nickel on the floor I thank God for the money. If I get a coupon that saves me a dollar I will thank God.

Steve

In Judaism, it is believed that the 27 letters of the Hebrew alpha bet (the "Aleph Bet") are 27 channels, or frequencies carrying sound, through which God created the world. It is also believed that the energy of your name has a direct bearing upon your life. It's why primordial Adam got to name the animals in Genesis. He had the gift of perceiving their true essence; thus their names carried that essence through the spoken word. It is so with everything...money and gratitude included.

Carole

Problem:

We take for granted those things in life that please us or make us happy. It's only during times of adversity that we turn to issue an acknowledgement of God/Source and issue a plea for divine assistance. We are not grateful and when we are, we *assume* there is no need to speak that gratitude into existence. Lack of gratitude or appreciation is a disincentive for the Universe to shower you with its bounty. When you add to that a belief that you are, in fact, unworthy you guarantee a diminished outcome.

Solution:

What words we use and how we use them matter. Literally. Therefore, how you speak about money and its Source determines what you are creating and in the end, what you receive. Remember, your brain and speech are tools, which when used as intended facilitate and expedite you receiving your portion of Creation. Further, gratitude is the acknowledgement that you are being *gifted* something... that the energy of money is flowing towards and through you because you have humility and appreciation in relationship to the Source of all abundance. When you express *gratitude in advance* of having received money, you are stating with certainty that what has not yet occurred in three dimensional reality has already, in fact, occurred in non-materiality... where all creation begins. Only time stands between Source's sending and your receipt thereof.

3. A Willingness to Receive

If someone offers to buy me a coffee I accept the offer, thank them and move on. I do this with everything from dinners to clothes to drinks at a bar. This approach is affirming my desire and ability to receive what the Universe is sending my way. If I reject small offers of money and kindness that come my way, how am I going to ever receive the large offers of abundance when they arrive? The funny thing is that as I open up my ability to receive, more comes my way. As opposed to accepting things out of a sense of false humility, I view it as a proxy of my ability to receive the Universe wants to send me. There's a story about a man who got stranded on his roof during a torrential rain storm. He prayed to God for a miracle and shortly thereafter, a small piece of wood appeared on which he could float to safety but he let it go by. Later, a small boat floated by but he passed on swimming to the boat as he was still waiting for the miracle. Finally, a man inn a speed boat came by offering his assistance and the man declined as he was waiting for God to save him. Eventually he drowned as rains consumed him and his house. As the man stood before God and inquired of God about his tragic death, God replied. "I sent a piece of wood, a row boat and a manned speedboat...what were you waiting for?" My experience has been that the Universe will provide me what I ask for...but the form and manner in which it comes might be different than what I had planned so I better be willing to receive it when it arrives.

Steve

My mother passed away in the same year that my ex-husband and I divorced. It was an extremely emotional and difficult time for me. As a result of my mother's estate and equitable distribution of our marital assets, I received two significant sums of money. As time passed and I had cause to spend some of the money, I did so but without allowing myself to enjoy it. In fact, I felt something akin to guilt and shame for having received it. As I focused upon the events that triggered the flow of money to me, both seemed very sad. I was confusing the earthly path of the money with the origination of all abundance, the God/Source. Once I allowed myself to receive the blessing, I was able to bring joy to how I used the abundance and, by so doing, was able to experience joy myself while bringing it to others through my gratitude and joyful intention.

Problem

Through incorrect teachings, both secular and religious, as well as dysfunctional parenting and socialization, we hold on to feelings of unworthiness. When you feel unworthy you simultaneously do not feel entitled to prosper by way of the abundance life has to offer. Diminishing your worthiness diminishes the value you will comfortably allow in to validate that self-worth.

Solution

Start with complements. Be aware if you reject or diminish complements or if you are open to receiving them. Release self-depreciating thoughts and feelings as they are a rejection and you and your entitlement to plenty. You want to set your energy field to a clear frequency of receiving. Whatever the Universe brings your way, from compliments to money, always accept it. Never say "No" by thought, word or deed. The more you are willing to receive, to allow the flow, the more the Universe will send money, things, and opportunities your way. The more you open your arms to "Yes" the more the Universe will fill that space with abundance.

). De-Clutter and Let Go

The less you own the less that owns you. Part of the crisis over the last few years has been the popping of the housing bubble and the long held American belief in home ownership. This myth was sold and fed to the public by the media and the banking sector. As more and more people bought houses at inflated prices, the inevitable bust left people with houses worth less with than the liens (mortgages) against them. For the people who were not able to walk away from that house, they have since found themselves tied to the property and making payments. For many, they can't move, sell their house or change their jobs. They are stuck. Even if a better job or opportunity were to present itself elsewhere, it would be unlikely they could move. The more weight and debt you carry around the harder it is for you to be nimble enough to attract the money that you need.

Steve

I recall once watching a special on TV about people who lived past the age of 100. It was based on a study of trying to determine what people from various parts of the world and various cultures had in common that allowed them to exceed that age barrier while still maintaining a sound mind and relatively healthy body. All possible variables were considered... local environmental factors, genetics, smoking, drinking, illness, diet, marital status and the list went on. In the end, the *only* thing each of those survivors had in common was their ability to let go of everything and anyone who was in their life who had been removed by whatever circumstance imaginable. Regardless of the cause, whether a loss was the result of death, relocation, job loss or an act of nature... it was their ability to let go while simultaneously appreciating and accepting what was gone. They turned their attention to the "now" of their existence, became re-engaged in their lives and allowed themselves to look towards the future.

Carole

Problem

From the tiniest fingers of a newborn baby grasping to wrap themselves around a comforting adult hand to the loss of a dearly beloved, we have a tendency to want to hold on. Wanting things to remain as they are is the antithesis of change and, therefore, Life. Life is about change and newness. It's about moving on not remaining stagnant. When we attempt to capture and imprison the present with the false expectation that we can stave off the changing future, we are attempting to defy the Laws of Nature, Humankind and the Universe. The attempt always fails and we are left trapped in our illusion.

Solution

Nature abhors a vacuum. Many people have trouble attracting what they want in their lives because they are clinging to everything... including their problems. Make a list of all the things you want to eliminate from your life then, one item at a time, take steps to eliminate those things. What you'll notice is that as you do this certain problems disappear as well. You begin to feel lighter, literally. In mind and body. Creating this new space, or vacuum, allows life to fill it with newness that is for your growth, highest good and best interest. Now you can magnetize something better to be pulled in your direction. As you eliminate those things you don't want… make certain you think and say "Something better is coming into my life now."

10. Create Vacuums in Your Life

When I want something, such as new clothes, I give clothes away. I go down to the local Goodwill and give them my old clothes. By doing this, I create a vacuum which I know will eventually have to be filled. And in short order I always get new clothes. My wife did not believe this process until she saw it in action firsthand. We had an amazing wooden dollhouse that over time had gotten banged up and was no longer as nice as it once was. I was certain that if we gave it away, someone would fix it up and they would be happy with it. Within 3 days of donating the house to charity, a neighbor called my wife and asked if we wanted a doll house. When she showed up the new dollhouse was newer and nicer than the one we had just given away. My wife's was astonished and now...she's a believer too!

Steve

I can't resist sharing a "vacuum cleaner" vacuum story. I have two cats. I also have two vacuum cleaners as I use one exclusively for the cat hair and utility room where their litter boxes are located and the other for the remainder of the house. The "feline" vacuum broke. Shortly thereafter, my oldest cat passed away. I was not going to get another but the cat that remained was so sad and unused to being alone that I was considering it when my Veterinarian phoned to ask if I would consider taking in a Burmese long-hair cat whose owners were relocating to Germany and were unable to take her with them. I was reluctant as I had never had a long haired cat and did not relish the idea of yet more cat hair. However, I felt sorry for the family and considering my cat's sluggishness I agreed. It turned out she was a beautiful, sweet feline. About a month later, her former owner called me to say they were about to leave for Germany and asked if I would like to have their new, $1200 Kirby vacuum. Forgive the pun, but the end of my vacuum created a vacuum, for the new vacuum, which was infinitely better than the one I had previously. It's a funny story but true. It's also how vacuums get filled when you're open to receiving what the Universe sends your way.

Problem

We get used to what we have. We take a certain amount of comfort, perhaps a disproportionate amount of comfort, in the familiar. We also tend to resist and even fear the unknown. These habits and feelings keep us from letting go and creating a space, or vacuum, where newness and growth can occur. We also live in a culture that lives by, and promotes, the adage, "more and bigger are better." So we acquire and keep on acquiring closing off the flow of change.

Solution

You can't fill up what was not first emptied. Neither can two things occupy the same space at the same time. Therefore, if you want to welcome change and embrace newness, you must first empty what now occupies the space you want to fill. Sometimes it's a conscious and deliberate emptying, such as Steve giving his clothes to the doll house away. But just as often it's the Universe making space on your behalf, as when my cat died and the new one appeared or the vacuum broke and the new one showed. So whether it's by design or default, know that all of materiality has a beginning and an ending. When the end comes, honor the vacuum it creates and anticipate the arrival of what is in your best and highest good.

11. Did They Say "Close the loo?"

In 2008, I started transitioning from Wall Street to the technology sector. Having worked in finance, sales and marketing I thought I would take the skills I had and apply them to my new field. I built many web sites and during that time I became quite familiar with the terms "a leaky site" and "tightening the web site." What these terms were referring to was keeping the customer engaged on your site and moving them along a deliberate path whereby they would by your product. Anything that stopped that flow of energy on the site needed to be removed. I have removed leaks on my web sites and literally seen the conversions increase by 400%! This could be accomplished by something as simple as removing a paragraph or changing one of tabs in the menu bar. What I find fascinating is that the Chinese are very familiar with static things having energy and by keeping the energy circulating, money and prosperity will come your way. So in the practical plane of life there is energy. But web pages have energy as well and can be optimized to eliminate leakage.

Steve

I am a licensed attorney but also a natural intuitive or psychic. I have been psychic most of my life. One of the things you learn early on in understanding the gift of intuition is that it's an energy transmission that can be hijacked by another, intentionally or unintentionally. Because different frequencies impact, interplay, or even interfere with one another, the consequences of having your energy depleted or hijacked can leave you feeling drained. It can also be the case that certain people sense your "frequency," or the vibratory rate at which your consciousness vibrates, and finding it appealing...more appealing than their own...seek to boost theirs by encroaching upon yours. Therefore, I learned the importance of energetically closing off those "openings" or points of potential leakage in my energy field so as to retain the energies that I receive from the God/Source.

Carole

Problem

We can't say it often enough. Everything, including money, is energy. When we have circumstances, things or people in our lives that cause us to "leak" our vital life force, we are disempowered. If you are not using energy correctly, when you oppose or try and circumvent the Law of Rightuseness™ you are disempowering yourself. That disempowerment can easily show up as insufficient funds.

Solution

Feng Shui, the Chinese system of harmonizing, can be instructive and enlightening. It provides specific guidance about most things in your home or office and how they should be placed or displayed. Toilets are no exception. At first this may sound not only strange but downright ridiculous. But think of it this way. If your home were a ship and the ship had a hole in it through which water could come and go, so to speak, how long before your ship sinks? Feng Shi teaches that closing the lids to the toiles in your house is akin to closing off the leaks of energy and prosperity from leaving your life. Remember, everything is energy! The energy of money needs to circulate in your house not leak out of it. So, even if you toss Feng Shui out the proverbial window, close off the energy leaks in your life be it toilets, people who drain you by taking without reciprocating, or perhaps by you not walking your talk because nothing leaks energy like inauthenticity.

12. Live The Dream

always carry money with me, cold hard cash not credit cards. Money is a magnet. The feel and touch of money becomes a trigger me all day long. If I encounter someone who needs cold, hard cash, I always have the ability to provide it. This is a great psychological trigger for me in that I always have the ability to say, "I have money." I never have to say I don't have money. Since being broke and being wealthy begin in the realm of ideas, I prefer to feed my mind with nourishing thoughts that I am wealthy. I even carry cash that I never spend so my knowing it's there affirms my belief that I have money. In addition, I make certain there are no images of poverty or lack on our walls. In fact, in my home office, I have a huge picture of a dollar bill that sits behind my head. It is a fabulous painting that reminds me every day what I am here to do. I am here to provide as much value to my clients as possible so that I, in turn, profit handsomely.

Steve

When I was attending law school, I commuted daily for two of those three years from Pennsylvania to Delaware. In order to avoid traffic delays, I learned all the back roads. In Delaware, those roads tended to meander through rural farmland. Each and every day I would drive past farms of expansive acreage with horses roaming inside "post and rail" fencing. How I loved the feel of that lifestyle and the look of those properties! I saw myself living in just that manner someday. Years later, married with a newly adopted daughter, my ex-husband and I were house-hunting. One day, I saw an ad in a local paper that read "Chester County Mini Estate" with a price within our range...which my husband thought must be a misprint as we could hardly afford an estate. Well, we went to look and, sure enough, there was the house and the land just as I had envisioned them a decade earlier. Plus, our few acres were surrounded by a conservatory trust of 400 acres so nothing could ever be built around our property. Upon moving in, the first thing we did was install the post and rail fence that completed the dream.

Carole

Problem

We tend to dwell on what we don't have or we repeatedly think about what we have... but would rather not have. All this does is solidify your expectations in the negative. In addition, the message you broadcast to the Universe regarding what is of importance to you is backwards. If you think about something repeatedly it must be really important to you. So, the message you broadcast and the picture you continually paint is one of dissatisfaction and failure.

Solution

Visualization and manifestation are powerful tools of creation. However, it's also important to *live* as much of what you desire *in advance* of you having it all. The place from where your prosperity derives has no time. It simply seeks to match your out-picture. So, when you keep money in your pocket at all times (regardless of your financial situation), surround yourself with images of abundance (regardless of whether they are in your life or not), or deeply and passionately feel the joy of what it will be like to achieve your goal (no matter how much time may be needed to get there)...you are actually laying the foundation upon which the completed structure can stand. Like attracts like, so immediately begin laying your foundation of prosperity so it will be able to hold the vast amount of money that will flow into it in response to your creation.

13. Gratitude

I have travelled to many countries in the third world and I have seen how poor people live. I have been in houses with no electricity, mud floors, no indoor plumbing, thatched roofs, and no refrigerator or washing machine. When I pray I always give thanks that I live in a house that has these amenities. Having been in the Marines and fought in the 1st Gulf War, I am always thankful that I came out alive and uninjured. In 2011, I was having a particularly bad year on Wall Street. I ran into a fellow Marine Officer one morning on his way to work who had lost his legs in a combat mission in Iraq. He was in a wheelchair but he was well-dressed and optimistic. What I noticed and admired most was his positive disposition. I knew from looking at him that he was grateful that he was alive and had survived such a traumatic experience. I left that changed meeting a changed man knowing how truly blessed I am. Whenever I feel depressed about life, I always reflect back on that Officer and his wonderful attitude.

Steve

My early life was driven by pessimism, worry and doubt. It was a long and at times difficult road arriving at optimism, faith and certainty but I made it. One of the ways I daily worried was at night in bed trying to fall asleep. In my mind, I would go over and over the day as it had unfolded thinking about all the things I should have done differently or what occurred that was bad or hurtful. I would inevitably get lost in feelings of anger, sadness, frustration and, of course, the inability to sleep. Then I discovered the concept of a "Gratitude Journal." At the end of each day, the last thing I do as I get into bed is enter into my Gratitude Journal all of the things (nothing is too small or too big) that happened during the day for which I am grateful. And while it is true that some days are more abundant with blessings than others, it's also true that no day is ever without blessings...even if the blessings are limited to not much more than food and shelter. Then, I put my journal on the night table next to my bed and easily go off to sleep filled with all that is good in my life.

Problem

Most of us like to gift something and receive some expression of gratitude or appreciation in return. If you keep giving to someone and they keep failing to show appreciation or gratitude...well at some point while you may not stop giving, you are likely to cut back on frequency or diminish the magnitude of your giving. In fact, you may even begin to think that what you are giving is not what they want at all which could, in fact, lead to your cessation. The Universe operates similarly.

Solution

Gratitude is a generating powerhouse! Your expression of gratitude is an incentive to the Universal flow of abundance to continue to flow in your direction. To the contrary, a lack of gratitude acts as a retaining wall, holding back the flow. You want to acknowledge and express your delight in receiving material blessings. Therefore, stop and literally say "Thank You" for the smallest sign of abundance. A penny found and the flow acknowledged is like turning up the spigot on a faucet. Increased flow follows.

14. Tip More & With Purpose

I use to work at the Hard Rock Café as a kid and would take care of the owner when he came to town. He was always super generous with his tips. The fact was he ran a tight ship but he also knew the more money he gave out the more money would come back his way... multiplied many times over.

Personally, I grew up in NYC. As a kid I noticed that my father always got first class treatment wherever he went. The reason was that he always tipped better than everyone else. In fact, I learned that Frank Sinatra was well known for giving $100 tips on a regular basis *long before he was super wealthy.*

Steve

In 1980 my family was eating dinner at a restaurant where we were vacationing. My father, always a charitable man, was being almost silly it seemed this particular night. Every time the busboy came to the table to fill up our water glasses, my father tipped him a dollar. By the fourth visit, you could see the busboy's confusion. He certainly liked the money but was probably worried that this poor man could not remember what he was doing. So finally the busboy said, "Sir, do you realize you have already tipped me...several times?" My father laughed and said "No problem, son. Enjoy it." When later in the meal someone who had witnessed and overheard the entire episode came over to the table to ask my father why he did that he replied as follows: "I don't drink, I don't gamble, I don't cheat on my wife. The difference between me and someone who tips sparingly is probably $2000 a year. Do you know how much pleasure I get for that $2000 and how much it means to the person receiving it?" My father never went beyond a high school education but became a self-made millionaire. I attribute it in no small way to his generosity and desire to help others.

Problem

We fear lack. It's an illusion but we fear it none-the-less. We are afraid to give money away because we think either 1) we do not have enough ourselves or 2) we will deplete ourselves of what we do have and when we need it...it will be gone. In resisting or even begrudging another our expression of gratitude for service rendered, we only perpetuate our belief in lack.

Solution

Be joyful, grateful and appreciative that someone else is in a position to provide you service when you need it. Show that appreciation with joy by tipping generously. Place the energy and the intention in your head that the money you tip for great service will come back to you exponentially. We suggest starting tipping 5-10% *more than you usually do* and start enjoying the effects right away.

15. Give Money Away

Dan Kennedy, serial multi-millionaire entrepreneur, always says "the hole that you give through is the hole that you receive through." So to receive more I learned I had to give more which I translated into "Steve, make a bigger hole!" Even if I think I have nothing to give, I check again. It might be books or clothing that I give away. By so doing, and feeling abundant about the process, that abundance is returned to me. In my mind I don't allow fear of non- return to stop me from giving. I don't think about it. If I withhold anything, I'm choking off the energy exchange flow. However, when I focus my attention on what I am giving *with joy and passion*, then passionate energy returns in the form of new abundance. Give first, receive second. If I'm lacking something, I remind myself that it could be because I'm not giving any of it away. So if its money I'm lacking then its money I give away and…sure enough… it flows back in ways I didn't even foresee.

Steve

grew up in a family and within an ethnicity that promotes *tzedakah. Tzedakah* is a fundamental part of the Jewish way of life. In fact, it's an obligation to do what is "right and just." In a Jewish home, it's not uncommon to find one or more "*tzedakah* boxes." These are ornamental "piggy banks" (if you'll excuse the non-kosher reference point!) placed about in the open. Spare change, and sometime larger bills, is deposited into the box. When the box is full, the content is emptied and given to someone or something in need. The poorest Jewish home may have a *tzedakah* box. Because *tzedakah* is so ingrained in my culture, giving seems part of basic existence. You give away clothing, furniture, money, time… whatever. You give it away because there is a fundamental understanding that when it comes to abundance, no matter how counterintuitive it seems, the first and highest action in being human is to give not receive. Physics has recently, and once again, caught up with metaphysics. We now know irrefutably, through controlled scientific studies, that the giver of charity or the doer of an act of kindness receives, by way of chemical release, a **larger quantity** of dopamine, the "feel good" hormone, than the amount of dopamine released in the body of the person receiving the largesse.

Carole

Problem

We open savings accounts looking for the highest interest rate. We invest in stocks hoping they'll go up. We purchase real estate and hope property values climb. We invest in mutual funds and life insurance policies hoping to maximize our gain. We buy lottery tickets and play slot machines hoping to strike it big. We must have the latest cell phones, computers and cars and are seduced into buying clothing and shoes we do not need because they're the latest and greatest. We spend a great deal of time and energy trying to increase the value of what we already have and amass more of what we don't. Sadly, you can't get anything of value unless you first give something away. We have it backwards.

Solution

Practically speaking, buy empty jars and place them around the house. When you have it, put small change in them. Over time you will see them fill up and you will be amazed, because you will literally see money beginning to "take shape" in your house. In addition, your mind will always be triggered and see money everywhere. As you move from room to room, money will be literally all around you wherever you go!

Let the money go. Let the money flow. It's energy, remember? If you bottle it up (not your jars but miserliness) and impede its movement you shut off not only the flow of money into your life, you actually negatively impact *all* the energy in your life. Periodically clean out your life. Look around. Spare money? Give it away. Excess clothing? Give it away. Books, cell phones, computers, knick knacks, time? Give them away. Everything you have has value and can be a joy to someone else...even if it no longer has value to you. And if you can't decide whether or not to let it go, ask yourself, "Do I love this? Does it uplift me and enhance my environment?" If the answer is no...show it the door

6. A Money Making Ideas Journal

I learned this from Author and Coach James Altshuler and I practice this every day. Every day I come up with 10 ideas on how to make money. Your brain is a muscle and it needs to be trained. If you lie down for a week after those 7 days you would not be able to walk because your muscles would have atrophied. And it is the same with your brain; it needs to be exercised and trained. When I first started, I started small. So my ideas were the following: start a dog walking service, house sit, and mow peoples' lawns. As I did this more and more my ideas became better and better. I became an idea making machine. Now when I have meetings with my clients I can usually look at about twenty things they have never thought of to improve their business. In addition, as I took time each day to record all the ideas I was generating, I was shocked how many *more* ideas started coming to me. I can tell you my consulting fees went up significantly after doing this because I could always find new ways for more clients to make money and...you guessed it... they would always come back to me.

Steve

I'd never heard of a "Money Making Ideas Journal" until I was writing this book with Steve. However, for as long as I can recall my mind is always looking at a situation or business and asking myself "How can this be done better, or simpler, or with greater ease?" I have what is called an "A" type personality....always on the think and always on the move. Someone once told me that even when I don't know the answer to a question my brain "goes on roam" and stays there until...maybe hours later...I'll suddenly blurt the answer out of seemingly nowhere. The point is that the Rightuseness™ of creative energy is key to living a successful and quite frankly, joyful life. So while I may not have a journal (although I like the idea and will probably start one now so "thank you" Steve) I've had the equivalent of a mental ideas journal all of my life. So, virtual or real it's a darn good use of energy.

Carole

Problem

We all have creative energy and we all have ideas worth remembering. The problem is that too often we've been made to feel that our thoughts don't matter. Or worse, that they are impractical, stupid or useless.

Solution

Recognize that your thoughts are like planting seeds in a garden. Not all seeds will take root. But for the ones that do, they'll need attention, nurturing and occasionally trimming. With the right nourishment and environment some will mature and one may bloom into something quite beautiful...even extraordinary. That one will be your show-stopping, award-winning masterpiece and "Voila!" you've gotten first prize at the fair. Now the recognition and abundance start rolling in.

17. Value Yourself

I read a great book called "Love Yourself Like Your Life Depends On It" by Kamal Ravikant. Kamal writes about the downward spiral that he entered into due to his business failings. He ended up gravely ill and in bed. The way he was able to self-heal and pick himself up again was by repeating the following mantra over and over, "I love myself." On the face of it, I was not very inspired that saying that mantra would help but on closer examination I actually think it is quite brilliant. Earlier in my career I actually worked for a short period of time with a former NFL quarterback who started for a few years but mostly was a backup. Our co-workers would forever tease him for a fumble he caused over 30 years ago. Instead of celebrating his talent and the hard work it entailed for him to become a professional football player, his peers focused instead on his one mistake. The assault on our psyches is tremendous in the world in which we live. Kamal's solution was simple; he re-programmed himself by reminding himself that he was loved. As you value yourself, you will attract the people into your life who will value you.

Steve

I once entered into a personal relationship with a man who was very charming. It took me quite a while to realize he didn't value me. In fact, he was envious of and intimidated by me but it was well masked by his charm. Over time, his devaluing of me was contagious and I caught it. Slowly, as I began to think less of my abilities and self-worth, my career took a turn for the worse and my income began to decrease accordingly. Once I released that person from my life and again became focused upon the uniqueness and value that was me, my life turned around and my career recovered... as did my income.

Problem

We live in a society that rejoices in tearing each other down. We also can attract people into our lives who are not only incapable of affirming us but who can intend to damage our self-esteem. Too often we enter into situations that do not support our highest good because we are really entering into a bargain whereby we are getting something we want...albeit at accost we unprepared to pay. Only when the bill comes due do we realize the error of our ways. You determine your value. If you place little value on your self-worth, that's exactly how much money will come your way.

Solution

Talk to yourself. We give you permission. It won't mean you're crazy, just determined to reinforce those qualities about yourself that are in your highest good. "I love myself." "I am creative." "I am successful." "I am able to give and receive love." Speak these sentences and any others that resonate with your intended goals. Say them out loud and often. Periodically check in with yourself to see if the people with whom you've chosen to surround yourself actually value you and are willing to exchange energy with you in meaningful ways.

8. Give More Than You Receive

In 1998 I was unemployed, married, with our first baby on the way. I only had about $1000 dollars in the bank and was living in one of the most expensive cities in the world. Some of the deals I had been working on had not panned out and I was desperate. In the mornings, I would go to church looking for Divine intervention and none was forthcoming. I was depressed. One day, while in church, I had this intense desire to make a donation. With only $1,000 to my name it was the hardest money I ever let go. I made a $100 donation to my church and, believe me, it was painful. There was no way I could tell my wife what I had just done. As I was leaving church I heard a voice as clearly as if someone were standing next to me say "be optimistic." Within 48 hours of making that donation, I got a call from a bank to trade for them. It was literally the dream job that I had been trying to get. I was blown away. I was suddenly gainfully employed with a terrific salary and benefits.

Steve

When I practiced law, I never thought about how much time and energy I gave to my clients or if I was billing for everything I was doing. Doesn't sound like your idea of a lawyer? I know. However, my concern was never how much money I was making but how much effort I was brining to attaining the best result for my clients. It was the norm for me to go above and beyond on all my cases. In fact, I had a reputation among my colleagues for being "everywhere doing everything all at once." Because my focus was the integrity of my work and not the financial reward, my only source of generating clients was referrals. That's all I needed! My clients liked me and appreciated my efforts on their behalf and so they recommended me to their friends. It was quite an accomplishment for a divorce lawyer. As for income, every year I practiced my income increased because the magnet drawing the money was the constant energy I gave not the hourly rate I charged.

Problem

We tend to look for the shortest and easiest way to get the job done without considering the highest good for all concerned. Expediency can be the death knell for integrity. We can also be too concerned with "what will I get out of it" and thereby put our focus on the compensation rather than the quality we bring to the task at hand.

Solution

Always ask of yourself a little more than you intended to give. Push yourself past that comfort zone and really seek to find and satisfy the "service" portion of what you are doing. No matter what the task or job, you can always find a way to make someone else feel that more than the work and or the compensation, you care about their experience and how the finished product or outcome impacts them.

19. **Be Aware of Your Relationships**

When I was newly married, my wife and I took a scuba diving trip to each get certified. Since I already had my license, I was working on upgrading my certification while my wife was learning to scuba for the first time. We went out in a small boat with 10 other people in very cold weather on a 4 day scuba diving odyssey. My wife struggled from the beginning as she had asthma which made breathing under water particularly difficult. In addition, English was her second language and at that time not yet very good...making it hard to understand the instructors. Most of those in her group were having a hard time passing the daily tests. They had to start every day with a 6AM morning dive in very cold water in a damp wet suit. Needless to say it wasn't very pleasant. She wanted to give up on numerous occasions. By the third day, four people from her group had dropped out. For the rest of the trip, her group continually complained about the experience, bringing the spirit of the whole boat down. On the last day, in order for her to pass the exam, she had to do a long swim in an area with whales nearby. Her fear got the better of her and she quit. As soon as she made that decision, the people who had already quit the training were quick to console her. They were happy to welcome in another failure and thereby validate themselves. When one of the girls said, "We're the failures from this expedition" my wife turned right around, jumped back into the water and completed her training. She was so offended by the characterization of her as a failure, as well as being associated with a group who saw themselves this way, she was instantly moved in the opposite direction which gave her the energy to succeed.

Steve

My daughter was a B or C student until 11th grade. That year I went through a divorce. She and I moved to a new house in a new school district. I was deeply concerned for how she would adjust having gone through the divorce and now confronted with all new people in a new school at such a delicate age. On her first day at the new school, she met a girl who asked if she wanted to sit with her at lunch. Knowing no one, my daughter was grateful for the invitation. It turned out the girl was part of the Honor Society and everyone at her table, boys and girls alike, were straight A students. They became my daughter's friends and social circle. At the conclusion of the first semester, and every semester thereafter, my daughter achieved straight A's. She had stumbled upon achievers and she wanted to be seen as their equal. That's all it took to cause her to excel.

Carole

Problem

There is a difference between liking and accepting people for where they are in life versus making them your closest friends or business associates regardless of their principles or values. Its error to think you can surround yourself with people whose values and standards are lower than yours and expect to survive the affect it will have on you.

Solution

Here are some quick tips:

- Get rid of friends who don't honor money.
- Tell me who your friends are and I will tell you who the man is.
  You are a sum of the 5 people with whom you spend most of your time
  You are a sum of the last 5 books you have read.
- A healthy person can't make a sick person better; but a sick person can make a healthy person sick.

The point of all of these is to remind you how your surroundings, especially the people in it, can and will affect you. If you are trying to make more money in your life and you are around people who repel or demean abundance, then get new friends. Be aware if you are growing as a person and your peers don't like the "new you." You can miss the fact that some may try and hold you back or tear you down because the new you reflects badly on them. Wish your friends well from your heart, but move on until they are ready to adopt a prosperity mindset. Find people with like values and embrace them.

20. Trust

I have a friend who is a psychic. When we first met she told me that I was a lucky man as I had dodged death on many occasions. Boy, did she ever get that right! When I was a child I was run over by a motorcycle, thrown in the air and landed head first onto the concrete. How I lived to tell the story remains a mystery. Later in life, when I was in the Marine Corps, I fought in the First Gulf War and actually had a bomb land a few hundred meters away from me. When I saw it, I knew I had to duck behind the LAV that was next to me. That bomb ripped into the LAV and took the brunt of the explosion and my life was spared. Yet another time during the war, my unit fired into a munitions dump to the left of me which suddenly exploded. I ducked inside the LAV and was lucky enough not to have my head blown off. I know now it was more than mere luck that I lived. In both the wartime events, I heard a voice inside my head telling me to move and duck. I believe that's how I survived. Had I not listened to that voice, trusted in it and acted on that prompting I would have died. Trust + Action = The Winning Combo!

Steve

Once I had to move out of the home I was living by a date certain. I had hired a mover, packed up the house but was unable to find a rental property in the price range I could afford. I went out almost daily with a Realtor but to no avail. As the move date approached, my friends began to worry. They asked me "Aren't you nervous? Scared? "No" I said, "It will all work out perfectly." One day my cell phone rang and the Realtor asked if I had time to look at property that had just come on the market. I met her at the house and as soon as she opened the door, I said, "Finally, the place I can call home." As I walked through the house it just got better and better. It had absolutely everything I was looking for and more, including a community swimming pool a stone's throw away that, it turned out, virtually no one used but me! I'm a swimmer and it was like having a private pool (with my own lifeguard!). By the way, that house materialized **4 days** before I had to vacate the property I had been living in. I never doubted for a moment that it would all end as perfectly as it did.

Carole

Problem

We're fearful. We misunderstand what fear is and how it's to be used. It's meant for life threatening moments in order to produce more adrenaline, cortisol and other hormones to make you faster, stronger and smarter in order to get out of danger. Other than that, it's useless…even destructive. We also doubt. It doesn't matter how great an idea is. As soon as you begin to doubt it, it's as if you've pulled the rug out from under yourself. Certainty is the cure. Have certainty in what you desire and what your goals are. Be certain that abundance is flowing your way even if you haven't received it yet.

olution

all it faith, belief, visualization or anything else that you like but it comes down to one word Trust. You ave to trust that Universe/God/Source **will** provide you with exactly what you need exactly when you eed it. Without that unwavering trust, it's impossible to let go and create the space to allow life to ring you abundance. Trust that outcomes will be in your highest and best interest.

21. Think Fast and Act Fast

The first time I met my wife I was 19 years old. I had gone to Ecuador to visit cousins and to spend some time with my family. She and I wound up at the same party and we hit it off right away. We spent the next few weeks together but when my trip was over, I went back to the US. I did not see her again until 10 years later. I had returned back to Ecuador and, through fate, saw her the first day I landed. As before, we hit it off right away. That was a Friday. I proposed to her the following Thursday and three months later we were married. It's now been 18 years since then and we have six daughters. When I saw her for the second time, I knew she was the person I was meant to marry. My wife told me she knew as well. How could either of us possibly have known things were to unfold as they did? But, none-the-less, somehow we did. Both of our families thought we were crazy and everybody thought the whole thing was a terrible mistake. Yet, I never once second guessed my decision. Even though many people tried to stop our marriage, I knew what the right thing was for my life and I acted upon that knowing. Had I waited or hesitated, my life would have ended up totally differently and without the blessings I now have as a result.

Steve

When I decided to go to law school I was living in suburban Philadelphia and had been out of college a few years. My grades had been good as an undergraduate at Villanova University. I took the LSAT's and had a respectable score so when I applied to Widener School of Law in Wilmington, Delaware I fully expected to be accepted. In fact, I was already making plans for moving to Wilmington in early September just before school was to begin. When the acceptance letter came I was shocked. I was offered "conditional acceptance" as I had been out of school for several years and would be required to participate in a Trial Admissions Program (TAP) that summer before the semester started. Only if I attained a "C or better average" would I be permitted to enter the first year class in September. TAP was starting 1 week from the day I received the letter! I never hesitated. I called my cousin, a lawyer who had an apartment near the law school, and asked if I could sleep on his sofa Monday-Friday in order to attend classes and use the law library. He said certainly. That's how I spent June, July and August that summer...sleeping on his sofa Monday to Friday and driving back to pack up my apartment in Pennsylvania on the weekends. I never hesitated nor did I think I'd be anything but successful in TAP. That instantaneous decision, which was totally outside the plan I had readied, allowed me to move into the lucrative practice of law I enjoyed for 14 years.

Carole

Problem

We get set in our thinking about how the Universe is going to bring us abundance. That mindset becomes a limitation that precludes us from acting spontaneously in the moment for our best and highest interest. It's our ego combined with our comfort level that gets in our way in those truly blessed moments.

olution

When Walt Disney first created Disneyland he saw it first in his mind and then transferred that image to the physical world. That's how creativity begins...as a thought. So when you are meditating on how to make money and a thought comes, act on it! Money is attracted to speed. Take some physical step towards turning your thought into reality. Even small steps count. Send an email. Make a call. DO something. Be the person that exhibits follow through. Before you can reap the benefits of a reaction...you have to take the action. Also, get comfortable being uncomfortable. If you master this concept, then when life asks that you act quickly in ways that you did not anticipate, you're ready, willing and able to move quickly. Practice courage. It's a muscle needing exercise. Regularly push yourself past your comfort zone in small ways so when the big ones come there's no hesitation on your part.

22. Release Your Financial Fears

I worked on Wall Street during the crisis of 2008. Given that most of my paycheck was tied to stock prices it was a very stressful time. Every day I had to realize I could lose not only my job but also all the savings I had worked for over a ten year period. In addition, since most of my clients were from Latin America, they no longer would trade with my firm because our credit profile was way too risky for Latin accounts .I literally lost 90% of my clients during the crisis when, at the time, it was more imperative than ever to generate revenue as the firm needed as much revenue as possible to survive. Every day I came into the office there were less and less people as the firm jettisoned employee after employee to bring down the burn rate. It was during these darkest of days that I started my technology company. I partnered with a friend of mine, got a lead investor and within weeks my business was up and running. Instead of focusing on fear or lack, I decided to move and create a new way to generate money. Six years later my business is still operational and the bank that I worked for is now part of Bank of America. Many of my former co-workers still have not fully recovered from that tragedy but it was my leap of faith during those dark days that saved me.

                                                                                                Steve

Having been raised in an affluent family, I never had concerns about money. My focus was never on thoughts that I might not have enough. I perceived money and life as infinitely abundant. That was my reality and my thoughts nourished that reality. Then I became involved with a person who worried about having enough money. He saw the world through the lens of how much money he had each day. His self-esteem was tied to how much money he was earning. His focus upon money, although he couldn't see it nor could I at the time, was on the belief that just over the horizon was looming financial lack. As we've discussed elsewhere in the preceding steps, your environment and the people in it can directly affect your flow of financial abundance. The longer I was associated with this person, the more concerned about money I became. It was a subtle but devastating shift in my consciousness over time. It was only when my financial resources had dried up and I witnessed myself worrying about money on a regular basis, that I realized I had taken on his fears and made them my own. When I jettisoned that person from my life, with him went the fear of lack and I returned to the mentality of abundance that had always been mine. Once again, my life became rich in every meaningful way.

Problem

Fear is immobilizing. It is the lowest frequency of human emotion because it shuts down your creativity and blocks the ability to receive Divine guidance. Even a small amount of it will proportionally obstruct your flow of abundance. IF you are faced with financial challenges and are fearful, you will not be open to receiving and manifesting the creativity necessary to resolve your challenge.

Solution

Begin to see that energy is a currency (*current* – See?) and if you have the right frame of mind, which entails allowing and accepting, you can enhance your currency of abundance. Use your mind as electric current uses a capacitor. A capacitor blocks direct current but allows alternating current to flow freely. Use your mind to block fear and allow abundance to flow freely. Meditation is the best way to dissipate and discharge your negative thoughts of lack... and any negative energy, generally. You can greatly increase your capacity to receive more abundance by abandoning a mentality of lack and embracing your creative capacity to generate and receive financial abundance.

23. Do One Thing Every Day. Build a Pipeline

My first job on Wall Street started out sending me to the farmlands of Iowa. The day I moved to Des Moines, I couldn't even enter the city because it was flooded. In fact the whole state was flooded with heavy rains and the corn crops were being destroyed by the moisture. My job was to buy as much corn as possible for the firm. I knew nothing about corn. The little corn the farmers had left, they didn't want to sell it to some trader who knew nothing about the commodity. I was left in a bind. I couldn't garner any trades yet I had to start producing. Without trades I would make no money. I did some research and found that damaged corn had value as a byproduct for feeding animals. I spent a few weeks finding out all the companies that bought damaged corn. I developed a spreadsheet of where I could buy the corn and where I could sell it, so that all the people involved in the transaction would benefit. My boss and my co-workers thought I was crazy! The general consensus was that farmers were not going to sell their damaged corn at bargain rate prices. Armed with my research and spreadsheet, I called all my accounts. By day's end, I had done dozens of trades. Soon thereafter, all of the traders on the floor started copying my strategy. Plus, word had gotten around the state that our office was buying damaged corn. The phone calls came in droves. No matter what the circumstances seem to be, do something every day to move towards your goals.

Steve

When I practiced law referrals were my bread and butter. I had satisfied clients and they referred me. But in the highly competitive world of divorce law, I also developed other aspects of my potentiality for income generation. I created a seminar for women going through divorce which I presented to live audiences. I wrote and produced a DVD version of the seminar then marketed it to QVC and sold it on-air. Every day I was involved in my practice, organization for the next live seminar or marketing the DVD. Every day my energy was directed toward maximizing the flow of income generation and, as I've stated previously, every year my income increased.

Problem

We often blame bad luck, poor timing, the economy or any number of external factors as to why we don't succeed. Rarely do we take responsibility for not having *consistently* invested enough of our time, energy and creative thinking in support of our goal. Your financial aspiration requires a driving force and since it's *your* aspiration...you're that force. Without you there is none.

Solution

Each day your focus has to be in building "a pipeline of business." The reality is that many of the things that you do won't work; it's a fact of life. Look at any endeavor in life and you'll see that failure part of the norm. Great baseball players only have to hit 30% of the time to be considered good. Basketball players only have to hit 40% of their shots to make the NBA. On Wall Street, the pros can lose 80% of the time and still be successful if they know how to limit their losses and ride their winners. So, your goal ould be making 10 calls a day, 10 emails a day, building that website or doing that research. But, you ave to move the needle every day. The natural state of things is atrophy or breakdown. If you were to e in bed all day you'd get weaker. If you just walked around and did some manual chores around the ouse, you may not gain strength but you wouldn't lose either. However, if you ran for 20 minutes a day r swam 20 minutes per day, your muscles would become stronger. The business cycle operates in the ame way. If you do nothing, your business will atrophy. If you do merely the basics, your business will tay the same. However, if you take consistent meaningful action your business will grow.

24. Count your Assets and Track Your Efforts

What you focus on grows. It is not what you *expect* it is what you *inspect*. I used to weight lift in my younger years. The only way I would get stronger was by constantly lifting a bit more than my previous workout. If I wanted to get stronger I had to track my results. I knew that if I did not monitor and take into account what I was lifting my results would be happenstance. It's the same with money. The wealthiest financial firms count their money every day. I took that as a cue and began to do the same. When I traded bonds for a living, I would count and recount my gains and losses each day. It was the only way I could measure myself and my progress. When I focused on making more money... I started to make more money.

Steve

I have a website (www.carolegold.com) and do a podcast two days a week called "Inspirational Gold." Steve and I have a website (www.abovethefraypodcast.com) and we do a podcast one day a week called "Above The Fray." Tracking listeners and visitors to those podcasts and websites is something I do several times a day. It's how we know how well we are doing at "spreading the word" and, ultimately monetizing our skills. I could just ignore the "back end" (statistical data) of what I am doing. However, if I want to watch and feed my growth I have to be on top of what that looks like or needs. I am no different with my back accounts and investments. I regularly monitor them to know exactly where I stand financially and what, if anything, needs my attention.

Carole

Problem

Sadly, personal responsibility and discipline are not at the top of our list as humans. These are qualities most of us have to want to develop and stay committed to. It's a whole lot easier to abdicate personal responsibility and throw caution to the wind when it comes to self-discipline.

Solution

Be courageous and honest with yourself about where you are at both financially and in your efforts towards growing wealth. Becoming the ostrich who buries its head in the sand will not allow you to see the picture of where you are and how close you are to getting where you want to go. It will, however, get you a mouthful of useless sand! If what you want is not sand but success and affluence, then you have to be willing to look reality squarely in the face. Yes, sometimes it difficult because we're far from our goal and what we see is bleak in relation to our goal. But, it's that honest willingness to acknowledge that distance and take renewed steps in the direction we're seeking to go that eventually get us there.

25. Program Your Brain for Abundance

When I was younger I would always doze off to sleep watching TV without caring what I dreamed about during my sleep. As I got older, I read many books on the power of the subconscious mind and how to get it to work for you. I learned how our conscious mind helps us manage the day to day, mundane decisions that we put on auto pilot such as brushing our teeth or driving a car. O the contrary, our subconscious mind takes in everything around us that our conscious mind can't process. That task would be too overwhelming for the conscious mind to process. However, our subconscious speaks to us through images, gut feelings, premonitions and thoughts that both warn us and help us. So instead of mindlessly going off to sleep with television, I began to ask my subconscious to work on problems that I needed to get resolved. For example, I once had a problem with a bad breakup with a girlfriend and, for some reason, I could not move on from that relationship. I asked my subconscious to resolve the issue and that same night I had a dream about a cat that was clawing my back and trying to suffocate me. I immediately awakened realizing what the problem was; I had to get the cat off my back! As a result of the images in that dream, and my paying attention to the message, I never thought about that relationship again. All I had to do was to stop thinking of her and the weight of the "cat" would be removed from my shoulders. Nowadays, I use my subconscious mind to program my mind to be aware of the pitfalls as well as the opportunities around me.

Steve

While Steve addresses this challenge through the sleep process, I do it through mediation. Specifically, Transcendental Meditation. About 6 years ago a good friend taught me the method. It took about 6 months, 20 minutes a day, before I began to see results but when I did they were undeniable! I let go of worry, stress, and nervousness then noticed how easily idea began to come to me to resolve issues in my life that were potentially problematic. As I combined mediation with my psychic abilities, I realized that I could set my intention for a particular answer or solution I was seeking, go into meditation, and receive that answer either immediately during the meditative state or sometime later in the day. For me, it's not been so much a process of training my subconscious to earn money as it's been a freeing up of those things that get in the way of creativity thereby allowing abundance to flow.

Carole

Problem

Our brains are like undisciplined children. Left to their own devices they will happily run amok. A brain amok usually dwells on what cannot be done rather than what can. Why? Well, we're not sure but since it's beyond the scope of this book the answer to the "why" isn't necessary.

Solution

What *is* necessary is to get your subconscious brain working for you rather than against you. You have to program, or re-program, it to assist you in reaching your highest good, not undermine you on the way there. Whether you ask your brain each night to provide you guidance in making money then record those dreams when they do (literally waking up and jotting things down in the middle of the night!) or use mediation to retrain your brain to be open to higher frequency transmissions that support your highest and best output, it only matters that you activate your subconscious to work for you. That's the seed level for the creation of money. With the proper soil and good seeds, prosperity will bloom.

6. Do Whatever It Takes

I once drove from Texas to California for a one day meeting. I couldn't fly because I did not have the money. I went to work for a year and half from 4AM to 6PM every day, which meant I had to leave my house at 3AM. That schedule completely upset my internal clock such that I walked around in a semi-comatose state for a year. However, everybody at work knew I would do anything to grow business. For example, I went to the Middle East during the start of the Second Gulf War because I was the only one of my colleagues who would go. My clients in the Middle East thought it was important to see their bank still committed to the region... so I went. My colleagues in the Middle East were so thankful for my being there that after the business trip was over, I ended up taking back an extra suitcase from all the gifts they gave me in gratitude. My clients as well as my superiors loved me because they knew there was very little I would not do for them to help grow the business

Steve

My success as a lawyer came from my willingness to do whatever it took within legal and ethical bounds to achieve my goals. My colleagues were often exasperated by my seemingly endless energy to go the extra mile. I once had a client who moved out of the marital home and left her dog in the garage of the house on the day it went to settlement. When I found out, I asked my ex-husband to drive to the property, rescue the dog and I then spent two days finding it a home. Another client's husband abandoned her and their two children, moved from Pennsylvania to Florida and claimed in the support hearing that he was destitute. But I had hired a private detective to collect the trash outside his home in Florida and found a wealth of information about all the money he was making and used it to cause him to commit perjury at trial. When I hired a PR firm and paid them $10,000 to promote my DVD on divorce and they produced nothing of value, I bought space at an International Women's Fair, designed, built and decorated my own booth which caught the eye of a Buyer from QVC walking through the event who picked up my product and put me on air to sell it.

Carole

Problem

We think some things are beneath us or too insignificant to be bothered with and so, we leave them to fate or happenstance. We want to work hard, but not too hard. We want the benefit without the burden. It defies the laws of Nature which is never a good plan.

Solution

Within the bounds of legality and morality, there should be nothing you would not do to further your desire to be financially successful When you put that message out to the Universe, and believe us the

47

Universe has "ears," it will heed your desire and fulfill it. Nothing should be too small or beneath you nor should you think it will somehow, miraculously, get done on its own. The fragile seed once planted has to push its way up through dirt, rock, roots of older trees, surface obstacles and defy the elements.

But it makes it none-the-less by exerting all its energy and doing whatever it takes. Miracles do happen.. but first you have to do your part, which is *everything you are capable of doing*.

7. Keep Your Person and Surroundings in Order

took Aikido for many years. It has been a great love in my life. However, time and injuries have taken their toll on me and I train infrequently now. Aikido has a multitude of moves and techniques that take years to master, if ever. In order to be good at Aikido, I had to work at mastering all of the simple techniques for years before I even started to understand what the more advanced movements were about. If you have ever seen an Aikido dojo, it looks as simple and unassuming as possible: clean white mats with a small shrine in front. Nothing else. But it's the simplicity of the space that allows the dynamism of Aikido to take hold. The movements are complex, varied and violent but they all begin with simplicity and cleanliness. In my fifth year of training, I finally understood what it meant to master simple moves. Had I not first focused on the basics, the complexity of Aikido would never have been open to me. I have worked out and trained with people who have studied Aikido for years who have never mastered it because they were searching for something deeper than the basics. I treat my money the same way; first the basics have to be mastered before any progress can be made. In Aikido, this was as simple as being a good follower on the mat and always having a clean uniform. With money, I always make sure my surroundings are clean, neat and I am careful that physical money I carry is in order.

Steve

used to be totally disorganized when I was younger. I paid no attention to how I treated personal property or where I placed my things. As a result, it was more common than not that I lost things or couldn't find what I wanted when I needed it. As I awakened to personal responsibility, I began to bring a sense of organization to my life. This included how I treated everything from my books to my money. As I became more organized and aware of how I treated my property, my life flowed with greater ease. It was certainly less stressful to know where something was than not know...or to have it in good condition when needed rather than neglected. But more importantly, I found that increased self-respect and confidence came with my willingness to be organized and thoughtful. Increased self-respect and confidence are cornerstones of making money.

Carole

Problem

Thinking that dirt and disorder do not affect us is reckless and an impediment to success. Drive around to the poorest area in your area and the things you will notice are always the same, garbage, graffiti, poor maintenance, unkempt lawns. Each one by themselves is minor but taken collectively they all signal a lack of care and a lack of money. The broken window theory is that if a neighbor breaks a window and does not get it speedily repaired, it's a signal to criminals that the area is not being taken care of. So a broken window can lead to graffiti which can lead to crime.

Solution

Money, when it shows up, is a "thing." How you treat your things says not only about you but it also signals to the Universe what you value. When you treat something (or someone) with disrespect it's because you do not value it (or them). This can even mean disrespect of self. When your living space, car or office space is dirty and disorganized you are not valuing yourself or that which you have acquired. Whenever you devalue through neglect you strengthen the message that you have no need for things of value in your life. Remember, money is a thing. Drive to the wealthiest part of town and you will see manicured lawns, clean houses, and well-lit streets. Again, taken by alone, they mean nothing yet collectively they mean a lot. Little things matter. Washing your car and vacuuming the inside is important. Brushing your teeth every day is important. Dressing well and appearing clean is important. These are all indicators of a consciousness of caring. So, tend to the small things and the abundance will follow.

In Closing

In his book "Mastering The Game" Neil Strauss writes about how to pick up women. At the time he wrote the book, Neil was writing for Rolling Stone Magazine and had been asked to do a story around "world of the pick-up artist." Neil wasn't handsome or funny and had never done well with the ladies. As he embarked upon interviews with these famous pick-up artists, he was expecting to meet a collection of Don Juans who were super handsome and super successful. To his amazement, what he found was just the opposite. Not particularly good looking or successful men... yet all of them had a surplus of girlfriends and women beating a path to their doors. Neil did a little digging and realized that all of these men fit a certain profile. Each had been outcast as youngsters having had no success with women. So to compensate for their loss, they studied the art of picking up and interacting with women. They studied with the same intensity that one would study any serious endeavor such as physics or law. Because of the effort and energy put into their studies, they got very good at implementing the techniques they learned. Neil recounts numerous stories of them picking up woman after woman in a variety of different circumstances. All of these men became successful at attracting and retaining the interest of women. However, *they all had to learn to master the inner game first.* They each discovered that if they could not create the energy internally whereby they perceived themselves to be handsome, successful and a good catch, they would never be able to pick up any women. The techniques of meeting and dating women would never work if first they did not fix their internal self-image.

Here is where the story gets interesting. What did Neil Strauss do after writing about these men? Well, he wanted to become successful with women in the same way so he fixed his inner game through meditation and programming.

The principles that Neil used to pick up women are analogous to the principles we have shared with you here in our book. No money will enter your life if your internal energy game is off. Your energy has to be grounded in faith and abundance before you will achieve the flow you seek. The pickup artists were not successful when they started. It was their willingness to fearlessly incorporate focused energies of dedication and practice into their lives that assured them their outcome.

It is no different with money.

If your energy is currently focused upon the condition of lack, realize that it's ok. Just get started on your internal game then adjust your external environment accordingly. Discover the Rightuseness™ for the energy of money and get started creating the abundance you deserve!

Steve and I want you to prosper. We are right there with you! We'd like to know how we've helped and how you are doing. Please share your stories with at contact@abovethefraypodcast.com.

ABOUT THE AUTHORS

CAROLE GOLD

I practiced law for 13 years because I came to it as a calling and not as a business. When the passion was gone so was my ability to make the commitment good advocacy requires. I left the practice in search of that same feeling of purpose that had drawn me to it. I found that passion in using my God given gift of intuition to provide hope and inspiration to others through mentoring, coaching, mediation and speaking

Having struggled myself through decades of confusion and depression, successfully masked by a "can do" exterior, I developed first-hand insights and solutions to overcoming adversity. It's sharing these insights and solutions that give me the utmost pleasure by fulfilling what I believe to be my life's purpose.

As a lawyer by training, I know the seduction of logic and precedent. However, not thinking for ourselves leads to enslavement and political correctness in the absurd... at which we've arrived. As Gandhi said, "Be the change you wish to see in the world." Be the individual in thought, word and deed that you were created to be.

There is only One of Us. The sooner we begin to fully comprehend out connectedness to one another, the sooner we can begin to repair the world.

Blessings, *Carole*

STEVE CLARK

I am the founder of Wall Street Grunt Investments and Local Magnet, a lead generation company based out of Austin. Over the past 15 years I worked in the financial industry as a commodities trader, bond broker, bond trader and salesman. The area that I mostly focused on was international finance in emerging markets.

Prior to my career in finance I was an infantry officer in the US Marine Corps and served in the 1st Gulf War. Given my background, I have a unique perspective on how the financial markets work especially as it relates to US foreign policy.

Given the enormous amount of upheaval that has taken place over the past few years, I hope to give our listeners a fresh perspective on the problems we are encountering today.

Steve

57030417R00033